The Economics of Energy

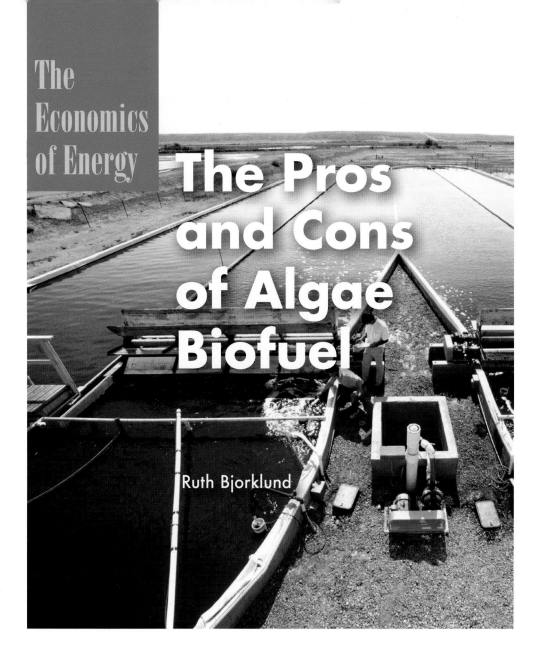

The Pros and Cons of Algae Biofuel

Ruth Bjorklund

Cavendish Square

New York

Published in 2016 by Cavendish Square Publishing, LLC
243 5th Avenue, Suite 136, New York, NY 10016

Library of Congress Cataloging-in-Publication Data

Bjorklund, Ruth, author.
The pros and cons of algae biofuel / Ruth Bjorklund.
pages cm. — (The economics of energy)
Includes index.
ISBN 978-1-5026-0954-0 (hardcover) ISBN 978-1-5026-0955-7 (ebook)
1. Algal biofuels—Juvenile literature. I. Title.

TP339.B64 2016
662'.88—dc23

2015027417

Editorial Director: David McNamara
Editor: Amy Hayes/Ryan Nagelhout
Copy Editor: Nathan Heidelberger
Art Director: Jeffrey Talbot

Designer: Amy Greenan
Production Manager: Jennifer Ryder-Talbot
Production Editor: Renni Johnson
Photo Researcher: J8 Media

The Economics of Energy

Table of Contents

Algae is one of the most basic and abundant forms of life on Earth. It holds great promise as an alternative energy source.

Chapter 1

Green Power

The United States consumed about 300 billion gallons (1,135 billion liters) of petroleum products in 2014, at a rate of about 800 million gallons (3,028 million L) a day. Highly developed countries, such as the United States and Germany, as well as countries that are the least developed, such as the Democratic Republic of the Congo and Haiti, all rely on **fossil fuels** to provide energy for their everyday needs. Fossil fuels heat homes and buildings, generate electricity, and provide liquid fuel to operate farm and manufacturing machinery. They power cars, trucks, buses, trains, and airplanes. As countries grow and expand, more and more energy will be needed. Studies based on reports from the former British Petroleum (BP) company suggest that if the world were to continue to use fossil fuels at the rate it does presently, it could consume all of Earth's known oil, coal, and natural gas reserves in less than fifty years.

Fossil Fuels

Fossil fuels were formed from the organic remains of dead plants and animals hundreds of millions of years ago. Five hundred million years ago, the Earth's atmosphere held eighteen times more **carbon dioxide** than it does today, creating a burst of **algae** growth. Algae grew for millions of years and afterwards died and sank into mud and rock. Over time, temperature and pressure compressed the algae and other plants and animals. The decayed organisms then changed form, becoming petroleum, natural gas, and coal.

Fossil fuels are non-renewable, meaning that once they are used up, they are gone forever. Besides the problem of their limited supply, when burned, fossil fuels pollute the air with carbon dioxide and other **greenhouse gases**. Most world leaders and scientists believe that these gases are leading to worldwide climate change. During the exploration, extraction, and transportation of fossil fuels, thousands of accidents, such as explosions, train derailments, shipwrecks, and oil spills, have caused serious damage to humans and to the environment. Furthermore, most of the world's oil reserves are located in the Middle East, a region of unstable conditions and conflict. The price of oil from these countries fluctuates widely. In response to these concerns, energy companies, research laboratories, and governments around the globe are investing in alternatives to fossil fuels. They all agree that new fuels need to be clean, abundant, renewable, and affordable.

Alternative Energy

There are many types of alternative energy sources, including wind, solar, water, and ocean power. The technology behind each of these energy sources is advancing rapidly. Homes and buildings have solar panels on rooftops that collect energy from the sun. Windmill "farms" are

Burning fossil fuels for energy is a major cause of air pollution, one of the many reasons scientists hope to develop efficient, non-polluting alternative fuels.

constructed on windy plains, mountain tops, and canyons. Hydroelectric power plants use energy from flowing rivers and dams, and new ocean power technologies make energy from the movement of waves and tidal currents. These sources generate power that feeds into the energy grid—the system of power plants and power lines that deliver electricity. However, not all of the world's energy needs take the form of electricity. Much of the world's energy needs are for liquid fuel. Some electric power plants run on liquid fuel and many people use liquid fuel as heating oil, but the greatest need for liquid fuel is to power vehicles and machinery.

Liquid fuels, such as gasoline and **diesel**, are made from fossil fuel oil. But sources of liquid fuel can also come from organic matter—plants and animals. These sources are clean, renewable, and abundant. However, the cost of converting these energy sources into affordable fuels is alternative energy's greatest drawback and the focus of much research.

Rudolf Diesel invented the efficient diesel engine, which originally ran on biofuel. His engine was quickly adopted and used in factories, boats, cars, and trucks.

A DEEPER DIVE

Rudolf Diesel, Visionary

A German refrigerator engineer named Rudolf Diesel conceived the idea of using biofuels to power machinery more than a century ago. In 1893, he was awarded a patent for an engine that was designed to run on vegetable oil. The design of his engine used pistons to compress air, making heat, which caused the oil to ignite and power the engine. He first exhibited his invention at the 1911 World's Fair in Paris. His engine was extremely efficient, of which petroleum companies took note. During the First World War, Germany powered many of its submarines and tanks with diesel engines using petroleum. It came to pass that the idea of biofuel to power Diesel's engine went by the wayside. Petroleum-fueled diesel engines became the standard. In 1912, Diesel stated, "The use of plant oils for engine fuels may seem insignificant today. But such oils may become in course of time as important as petroleum and the coal tar products of the present time."

Biofuels

Fuels that are made from plant and animal sources are called **biofuels**. Biofuels can come in the form of biogas, **ethanol**, and biodiesel. Animals were some of the earliest sources of fuel, as human ancestors burned animal fat, such as whale and seal blubber. Today, animal-sourced fuel comes from processing the waste of livestock—cows, pigs, and horses. The process produces methane gas. Animal fats and oils that are by-products from processing meats are also a biofuel source.

Plants are by far the most efficient and available source of biofuels. Plant sources of biofuel include algae, soybeans, corn, sunflowers, sugarcane, and potatoes. Biofuels made into ethanol, a type of alcohol, come from plants that produce sugar such as sugar beets and from grains such as corn. Biofuels made into biodiesel come from the oil found in plants and vegetables such as algae, soybeans, and peanuts. Both biodiesel and ethanol can be blended with traditional fossil fuels to produce liquid fuels that reduce consumption of fossil fuels and cause less harm to the environment. Biofuels can also be used as a stand-alone fuel in specially engineered vehicles and machinery.

Algal Biofuel

The US Department of Energy believes that algae is unique among plants that produce biofuel. Government researchers cite algae's many advantages over other plant sources, including its ability to grow in a variety of climates and conditions, as well as its ability to grow quickly. Algae biofuel, also called algal biofuel, is considered to be easier to convert to energy than many other plant sources and releases fewer harmful emissions into the atmosphere.

What Is Algae?

Algae is a group of mostly aquatic organisms that range in size from microscopic, single-celled organisms to large seaweeds, such as giant kelp. Ironically, algae contributed to the forming of fossil fuels. Ancient algae plants died, their decayed remains became embedded in rock, and through pressure and heat over time, they turned into petroleum. Much of algae's chemical composition is very similar to that of petroleum. Algae is made up of proteins, carbohydrates, and **lipids**. Lipids are vegetable oils. Some algae are as much as 60 percent lipids. Algae plants grow in an enormous variety of environments, and require only water, carbon dioxide, and sunlight.

The History of Algal Fuel

In 1937, Hans Gaffron, a German scientist, escaped Nazi Germany and fled to the United States. He set up his research laboratory at the University of Chicago. There, he investigated algae as a fuel source. He saw that algae could produce hydrogen, a gas that can be used as fuel. Most of the research following Gaffron's was devoted to producing hydrogen from algae. The next step was taken in the 1950s, when researchers at the Massachusetts Institute of Technology and the University of California at Berkeley began studying algae as a potential alternative to oil-based fuels. In some of their experiments, they grew algae in wastewater treatment ponds and processed it to produce biogas from methane. The projects were abandoned as research began to focus on large-scale programs to develop food crop–based biofuels that could compete against the efficiency and availability of fossil fuels. In 1970, the United States passed the Clean Air Act, allowing the US Environmental Protection Agency (EPA) to regulate emissions of air pollutants such as carbon monoxide, sulfur dioxide, and ozone and nitrogen oxides. The regulations encouraged development of cleaner burning fuels and allowed additives to petroleum fuels such as ethanol and biodiesel.

From 1973 to 1974 and again from 1978 to 1979, the United States and much of the rest of the world suffered from major energy crises because of conflicts in the Middle East. The price of gasoline and heating oil skyrocketed in the United States. The government took action by supporting the research and development of alternative energies, including biofuels. In 1978, President Jimmy Carter established the Aquatic Species Program (ASP) run by the National Renewable Energy Laboratory (NREL) to research algae as a possible replacement for fossil fuels. Many researchers concluded that if produced in large enough amounts, algal biofuel could provide the nation with its home heating and transportation needs. Large-scale research continued until 1995, when the government's biofuels program turned its attention toward ethanol production.

Development of algal biofuel did not end, however. In 1998, the government passed an amendment to the Energy Policy Act (EPAct) allowing for the use of biodiesel, including algal biofuel, in government-owned diesel vehicles. In 2007, Congress passed the Energy Independence and Security Act, which puts policies in place to produce "clean," renewable fuels, increase efficiency, decrease reliance on

A laboratory researcher at the Pacific Northwest National Laboratory checks algae growth in an experiment using light emitting diodes (LEDs) instead of sunlight.

A Timeline of Algal Biofuel

1893 Rudolf Diesel designs engine that runs on biofuel

1939 German Hans Gaffron researches algae as a source to make hydrogen fuel

1950s University researchers grow algae in wastewater to produce methane gas

1970 Passage of the Clean Air Act

1973–1974 Arab Oil Embargo drastically reduces supply of Middle East oil to the United States

1978–1979 Iranian Revolution interrupts supply of oil and prices skyrocket for foreign oil

1978 President Carter establishes Aquatic Species Program within the Department of Energy's Biofuels Program

1978–1996 Government scientists research algae as potential replacement for fossil fuels

1995 Decision for government biofuels program to focus on ethanol

2007 Energy Independence and Security Act passes Congress

2007 Congress authorizes ARPA-E program, funding many algal biofuel research projects

2009 Algaeus, an algae-powered Toyota Prius, crosses the United States getting up to 150 miles per gallon (64 kilometers per liter)

2015 Algae-based jet fuel produces 68 percent less greenhouse gases and is certified by the US EPA as an "advanced biofuel."

foreign oil, and to promote research into alternative fuels. Also in 2007, Congress authorized the development of the Advanced Research Projects Agency (ARPA-E) within the US Department of Energy. The agency funds advanced research into new energy technologies. Since its start, it has awarded millions of dollars toward research in algal biofuel.

Beyond US government involvement in algal fuel research, privately owned factories, laboratories, and businesses are expanding in the hopes that by producing enough affordable algal biofuel, the United States and other countries can end their reliance on fossil fuels. However, before this goal can be achieved, there are numerous obstacles to clear along the path toward energy independence.

Overall, the research of algae biofuels is promising. In 2012, the Environmental Protection Agency declared that algae-based diesel reduced greenhouse gas emissions by more than 50 percent compared with conventional diesel. That same year, the Obama administration awarded $80 million in research grants to study new technologies in algae-based biofuels.

CRITICAL THINKING

- Can you think of some limitations that alternative energies such as wind, water, and solar power production face? How would you compare their drawbacks to algae-based biofuels?

- What are some of the reasons countries shouldn't rely on fossil fuels for energy? Do you think algae biofuel sounds like a good alternative?

- Do you think that the government should invest in algal biofuels or should only private companies bear the costs, as they will make the profits? Why or why not?

Japanese businessmen look over a state-of-the-art algal biofuel production facility. Research into growing algae for fuel is rapidly expanding around the world.

Chapter 2

Algae to the Rescue

Supporters of algal biofuel say that converting algae into biodiesel is the best and most promising solution to end the world's dependence on fossil fuels. In 2014, the United States consumed 3.26 billion **barrels** (136.78 billion gallons or 518 billion L) of gasoline and diesel fuel, with a daily average of nearly 9 million barrels (375 million gal or 1,420 million L). There are more than 270 million cars, trucks, motorcycles, and boats in the United States. In 2015, the US EPA set standards requiring that 9.6 percent of all fuel consumed by vehicles in the United States should be renewable fuels, including 1.9 billion gallons (7 billion L) of biodiesel.

Ethanol versus Biodiesel

Ethanol is the most widely used biofuel in the United States, and is available at gas stations nationwide. The standard ethanol-gasoline mixture is called E10, or 10 percent ethanol and 90 percent gasoline. Most vehicles do not perform well if the percentage of ethanol goes beyond 20 percent. However, ethanol blends can be used in any gasoline-powered engine without any adjustments. Most ethanol is made from corn and sugarcane. When ethanol is burned in a vehicle, the level of carbon dioxide in exhaust emissions is much lower than standard gasoline, but an ethanol mixture produces 30 percent less power. Biodiesel is a more powerful and efficient biofuel. So why is ethanol so popular? The cost of making ethanol is 20 percent less expensive than biodiesel, although it uses more energy to process. Biodiesel is made from oily plants, such as soybeans, algae, and seed plants like sunflower and safflower. It can be blended with petroleum diesel to work in any diesel engine. With only slight modifications, a diesel engine can also run efficiently on 100 percent biodiesel. A study by scientists published in the magazine *Bioresource Technology* concluded that algal biodiesel can reduce toxic carbon dioxide (CO_2) emissions by 50 to 70 percent. Algae is most often made into biodiesel, but after processing, its by-products can also be made into algae-based ethanol, making algae the cleanest and most renewable biofuel source.

How Algae Grows

Algae simply needs sunlight, water, and carbon dioxide to grow. Algae uses the **chlorophyll** in its cells (the green pigment in plants) to convert sunlight into energy. Algae also absorbs carbon dioxide from the atmosphere, and through a biological process called photosynthesis it mixes sunlight and carbon dioxide into sugar to make its food. Some algae makes more food than it needs and stores it as fatty acids, or oil (as humans and animals store fat).

Carbon dioxide is created when humans and animals breathe out, but it can also be released in harmful quantities by burning fossil fuels.

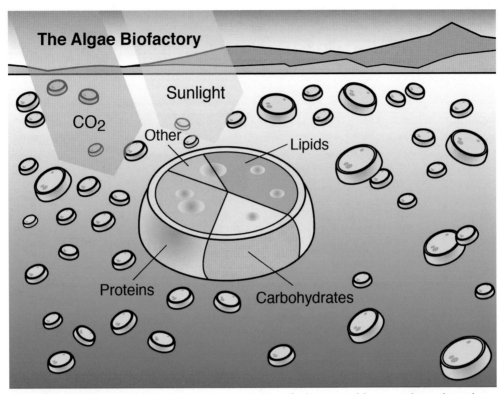

The Algae Biofactory

Sunlight

CO_2

Other

Lipids

Proteins

Carbohydrates

This diagram shows the biochemical makeup of algae and how carbon dioxide and sunlight are used by algae to grow quickly.

Carbon dioxide, along with methane and other gases, collect and form a layer in the Earth's atmosphere. Sunlight passes in and out of this gaseous layer. However, if the layer is too thick, too much sunlight is trapped, causing a "greenhouse effect" that disturbs Earth's climate. Algae is not only beneficial as a fuel source, but by absorbing carbon dioxide, it is also capable of cleaning polluted air caused by burning fossil fuels.

Given the right conditions, algae grows extremely fast, often doubling in size several times a day. Not all species of algae grow in the same

Comparison of Biofuel Sources: Algae versus Corn, Sugar, and Sugar Beets

ALGAE

- Does not need soil
- Does not require fertilizer
- Can grow year-round in containers
- Can grow in wastewater, salt water, or fresh water
- Can be harvested daily
- Refining process uses less energy
- Produces 10,000 to 20,000 gallons of fuel per acre (93,500 to 187,000 L per hectare)

CORN, SUGAR, AND SUGAR BEETS

- Require large tracts of agricultural land, taking away land once devoted to food crops
- Require fertilizers, which can lead to water pollution
- Require a long, sunny growing season
- Must have fresh water, adequate rainfall, and/or irrigation
- Heavy farm machinery uses large amounts of fuel to harvest annual crops
- Refining process is longer and uses more energy
- Fuel production per acre: corn, 354 gallons; sugarcane, 662 gallons; sugar beets, 714 gallons (per hectare: 3,310 L, 6,190 L, and 6,676 L, respectively)

way. Some produce more carbohydrates while others produce more lipids. Scientists estimate there are more than 72,500 species of algae. But researchers have been able to hone in on some of the most suitable species for each type of growing condition. Some species of algae are more than 60 percent fat—and the oil closely resembles petroleum crude oil as it is pumped out of the ground.

Algae Farming

Algae can be grown just about anywhere—in freshwater ponds, saltwater marshes, brackish aquifers, waste treatment holding ponds, and "grey water" tanks (grey water is wastewater that comes from the laundry, kitchen, bathroom faucets, baths, and showers, versus other wastewater, which comes from the toilet and garbage disposal). Growing algae in shallow open ponds or trenches is the easiest method, but it's not perfect. Because they are uncovered, there is less control over the amount of sunlight and water the algae receives. Also, it is sometimes difficult to prevent unwanted organisms or bacteria from contaminating the ponds. In some ponds, the upper layer of algae can grow so quickly that it blocks sunlight and carbon dioxide from reaching algae growing underneath. To solve this, growers use a system of pipes that churn up the water so that algae growing underneath can come to the surface. Other farmers cover their fields with a clear barrier, forming a giant greenhouse over the ponds. This has many benefits, such as trapping more heat, preventing contamination, and extending the growing season.

Many growers opt to grow algae in vertical farming systems that take up less space and use 20 percent less water than other farming methods.

There are several highly productive species of algae used to make biofuel. The open pond algae farm above uses a blue-green algae called spirulina.

In the field, farmers wrap the vertical structures in plastic sleeves that trap sunlight and prevent contamination.

Another way to grow algae is in large containers. In a container system, the grower must provide all of the algae's needs. Sunlight is provided through special lighting panels and carbon dioxide is pumped into the containers. In some systems, sugar is added directly, providing food to the algae and bypassing the need for sun lamps and carbon dioxide pumps. The algae in the containers must be watered. However, the watering system can be carefully controlled and the water can be recycled back into the system. The water does not need to be fresh water. Another type of growing system uses what are called **bioreactors**, which

The National Renewable Energy Laboratory in Colorado experiments with several methods of growing algae for biofuel, including this "tent" reactor.

are transparent aquariums hung vertically from the roof of a greenhouse. The algae receives sunlight from both sides of the hanging aquarium, and since the bioreactors are closed, no other organisms can enter. Still another type of system runs on photo-bioreactors. These bioreactors also stand vertically and, like containers, do not receive natural sunlight or carbon dioxide. Instead, special lighting panels are used, and carbon dioxide, water, and other chemicals, as well as sugars, are pumped in. A senior scientist at NREL said that by using photo-bioreactors and by blending in sugar and other substances, "We've almost doubled the fuel we can get out of the same amount of algae." The container and sugar

Algae is sometimes grown in water treatment plants. The algae feeds on the contaminants in the wastewater and later the algae can be converted into biofuel to provide energy for plant operations.

method for growing algae works well in environments where plentiful water and/or sunshine is not available, such as in deserts, rain forests, or areas with extreme temperatures. By being able to thrive in a wide range of habitats without needing to consume fresh drinking water or requiring large expanses of fertile soil, algal biofuel promises to be the best chance of bringing safe, clean, renewable energy to all regions of the world.

Some algae grows in salt water. Although there are many saltwater species of algae that are tiny, mostly large algae, such as kelp, are used to produce biofuel. Seaweed and kelp are often simply tied to large floating lines and allowed to grow along the shore. Saltwater algae does not need fresh water to grow and produce oil. One of the largest algae biofuel companies grows its algae for jet biofuel in salt water.

Some communities are experimenting with growing algae in wastewater treatment ponds. The algae is also able to absorb many of the unwanted chemicals in the sewage, such as **nitrogen** and **phosphorus**. The first major project in 2009 produced more than 150 tons (136 metric tons) of algae from just 15 acres (6 hectares) of sewage ponds. The algae is also able to absorb CO_2 emitted from the nearby treatment plant. In this instance, algae serves a dual purpose: it is being grown for fuel as well as assisting in cleaning up wastewater and toxic emissions from a treatment plant. A recent study conducted by the Department of Energy's Pacific Northwest National Laboratory (PNNL) states that the nation's land and water resources could support the growing and processing of enough algae to produce up to 25 billion gallons (95 billion L) of algae-based fuel a year in the United States.

Harvesting Algae

The algae harvest cycle is from one to ten days. Scientists at the NREL laboratories say they "harvest every other day." There are many ways to harvest algae and new methods are being studied. One of the most inexpensive processes pumps bubbles into ponds growing the tiniest algae, called microalgae. The bubbles separate out the fattiest algae

Algae commonly is separated from water in a spinning centrifuge. After the algae is scraped from the centrifuge, growers reuse the water to grow more algae.

and lift it to the surface where it can be skimmed off. The most commonly used method is an algae **centrifuge**—a machine lined with superfine filters that spins rapidly and forces water out. The algae is scraped off the filters and the water is recycled back into the grow ponds. Certain natural chemicals, such as lime or ground up seashells, can also be mixed into algae ponds. The chemicals cause the algae to clump up, making it easy to collect. In a method called froth flotation, air is forced into the water, making it foamy. The algae floats on top of the foam and is skimmed off.

Processing and Refining Algae

Of all the biofuel sources, algae-based biofuels are the most similar to petroleum-based fuels, especially petroleum extracted from under the ocean. Petroleum oil from under the sea was formed from seaweed millions of years ago. Because of this

An employee at Sapphire Energy in California checks algae samples. Her company produces algae that goes into making biodiesel for cars and trucks as well as jet fuel.

A DEEPER DIVE

Negative as Positive

Algae has more benefits than other alternative energy sources. All fuels, most especially fossil fuels, release carbon dioxide when they are burned. The amount of pollution that these fuels create is measured by what is called a **carbon footprint**. A carbon footprint measures how much the fuel-burning activity (such as operating cars, coal-burning power plants, or factories) impacts the atmosphere. There are a growing number of regulations and requirements that are being placed on vehicles and industry to reduce that carbon footprint. Most activities are expected to strive for a "carbon-neutral" footprint, meaning that whatever carbon dioxide (and other greenhouse gases) the activities release into the atmosphere, they must offer an equal reduction elsewhere. Examples include conservation programs, sponsoring environmental projects (such as planting trees, which absorb carbon dioxide), or buying credits from companies that are working toward reducing CO_2, such as windmill or solar panel companies.

similarity, much of the "crude" oil extracted from algae can be processed in the same processing facilities used to process petroleum oil.

Scientists have developed many mechanical and chemical methods of processing oil from algae. The most common form is called expression, which is simply a process of pressing the oil out of the algae, just as olives are pressed to make olive oil. There are several types of presses, each designed to process different types of algae. Eighty percent of the oils in algae can be retrieved by the expression method.

Another method is much faster—**ultrasonic** processing. First, a liquid solvent (a liquid used to dissolve another substance, such as dish soap that breaks down cooking grease) is added to a batch of algae, and ultrasonic sound waves are pumped in, which form bubbles in the solvent. When the bubbles burst, they crack open the algae cells, releasing their oil. Several

Algal biofuel is in a unique position. While algal biofuels do release CO_2 when they are being processed and later burned, algae is capable of absorbing more CO_2 while growing than it will release. Additionally, algae farms can be built alongside algae processing plants, reducing transportation costs and absorbing the CO_2 emissions from their own refineries. These qualities actually make algal biofuel "carbon-negative."

other methods use various different chemicals to release oil from the algae. By using a combination of expression and chemicals, processors are able to extract an amazingly efficient 95 percent of the oil in the algae. The oil extracted through these methods is called "green crude." It is not yet ready for use as fuel, but as it is so similar to fossil fuel crude oil, it can be refined.

Algae can produce more fuel than biodiesel. Not only is it fast growing and high in oil content, but its non-lipid (non-fatty) parts can also be used to make fuel. Once the oil is extracted, the cell walls, chemicals, and leftover sugar in the algae can be processed into algal ethanol, a clean-burning alcohol that can be used as a stand-alone fuel or mixed with other fuels. Other by-products from algae processing are chemicals and minerals that can be used to produce electricity, natural gas, and fertilizer to grow more algae. Taking advantage of producing all these renewable energy products, *Smithsonian* magazine reports that government scientists believe the cost of algal biofuel could become as low as $2 per gallon ($0.53 per L) in the near future.

On the Road

Fortunately, the money being invested in algal biofuel by governments and businesses is not all going into laboratories. Large-scale algal farms are growing and producing algal biofuel and the fuel is being used to operate vehicles and machinery. In New Mexico, one of the leading algal biofuel companies surpassed its goals and produced 81 million tons (73.5 million metric tons) of algae in its first year. The processing facilities are on a 300-acre (121 ha) farm, allowing the company to recycle water and reabsorb CO_2 emissions.

A Toyota Prius named the "Algaeus" used a hybrid blend of algae biofuel to drive across the United States on just 25 gallons (95 liters) of fuel.

Refineries today are able to produce algal biodiesel for vehicles, trains, and machinery, as well as jet fuel for aircraft. Most other biofuel sources are refined into ethanol, but ethanol cannot be turned into oil-based fuel without taking on many additives, including petroleum. An algae researcher at Brooklyn College states, "Converting algae doesn't need special handling or blending. We cannot fly planes with ethanol. We need oil." In 2011, a United Airlines Boeing 737 flew passengers from Houston to Chicago using a blend of jet fuel and algal biodiesel. The US Navy has flown its F/A-18 Hornet fighter jets using a blend of 50 percent jet fuel and 50 percent algal biofuel. In 2009, a Toyota Prius gas-electric hybrid car drove across the

A DEEPER DIVE

Lurking Under the Bed

In 2013, when Sara Volz was a seventeen-year-old high school senior, she made big ripples in the science community for her work on algae as a biofuel. She won the $100,000 grand prize given by the Society for Science and the Public in a nationwide high school research competition. During the ceremony, she was honored by the society's president, who said, "Sara's research on a novel method to help make algae biofuel economically feasible has the potential to make a serious impact on a critical global challenge."

Where was Volz's laboratory? Under her loft bed. There she kept watch over vials of algae grown in solutions. She needed to monitor the algae frequently, which is why she chose to construct her state-of-the art laboratory in her bedroom. She slept according to the same light cycles that the algae used. On a much smaller scale, she used many of the technologies used by algae growers. She forced bubbles into the vials to stir up the algae so it all had equal access to sunlight as well as plentiful CO_2. Her observations and detailed

recordkeeping highlighted what would become the most efficient and strongest oil-producing algae to date.

Volz's breakthrough was the discovery that a herbicide (plant-killing substance) mixed in with the algae could prompt certain algae to create more oil than normal. Her theory was that because algae needs oil to survive, only the strongest and highest-volume oil-producing algae could combat the attack of the herbicide. Basically, it was a "survival of the fittest" experiment. After concluding her experiment, Volz said, "When I first saw these results, I thought they were too good to be true." But they are true, and the algal biofuel industry as well as the rest of the world will likely thank her for her hand in giving the world a clean, affordable, reliable, and efficient energy source of biofuel.

country running on a blend of algal biofuel. The car used only 25 gallons (95 L) of fuel to go more than 3,000 miles (4,828 km).

In 2012, California began a pilot project in four cities, allowing certain gas stations to sell a blend containing 20 percent algal biodiesel to consumers. They reported that the biofuel mixture was more efficient and had reduced the emissions of standard diesel-driven cars. The gas stations had a 35 percent increase in sales and most consumers reported that they would prefer to buy algal biodiesel rather than standard diesel for their cars. The president of the gas station company said that they "were thrilled to enable our customers to be the first in the country to purchase this next generation biofuel." Today the company is expanding and now has more than forty-five stations that sell algal biofuels.

A company in Florida is constructing an algae biofuel plant to make fuel for airplanes as well as for ground-based vehicles. It has already successfully tested a jet that can fly on 100 percent algal biofuel. The company president believes that with more research in the near future, algae-based biofuel could replace petroleum without any changes to present-day engines.

CRITICAL THINKING

- Do you think buying or trading for carbon credits is a good idea? For the short term? For a long-term solution? Should algae farmers and processors sell their carbon credits? Why or why not?

- If you were buying a new car that you plan to keep for ten years, would you be more or less likely to buy a diesel car? Why or why not?

Algae is the most abundant and
fastest-growing source for biofuels,
but only a few species produce large
quantities of oil efficiently.

Chapter 3

Bumps in the Road

While many agree that a fast-growing and energy-efficient fuel could be a boon to societies around the world, many experts are very cautious. The algae industry has suffered "fantastic promotions, bizarre cultivation systems, and absurd productivity projections," according to John Benemann, PhD, a biochemist who worked in the Aquatic Species Program for the US Department of Energy. Dr. Benemann goes on to say that algae biofuel is expensive to produce, whereas fossil fuel prices are comparably low. He says that the only advantage of algal biofuels is that "an oil field will deplete eventually, while an algae pond would be **sustainable** indefinitely."

The economics of producing algae biofuels weigh down the positive aspects of clean, renewable energy produced from a fast-growing and oil-rich plant source. There are serious issues of cost in every stage of algal biofuel development and use—in growing, harvesting, producing, researching, and paying to fill a vehicle's fuel tank.

In the Field

It may appear that algae's needs seem basic, but many energy experts say there are many concerns and many more obstacles to overcome before algal fuel can be produced effectively. Out of tens of thousands of species, algae growers must choose the right species for their planned growing environment. They must also choose whether to grow the most oil-producing algae or an algae that produces less but costs less to maintain.

The least expensive environment is open pond growing, which is not without costly hurdles. Outdoor growing requires sizeable tracts of land for fields, ponds, trenches, greenhouses, and other facilities. Ponds and trenches take up a lot of space because growing algae needs more water surface, not depth. Sunlight only reaches the algae on the upper layer of the pond, so the water needs to be stirred up, usually by pumping in bubbles or creating water currents. Again, this adds cost to the system. Furthermore, in order to grow algae efficiently outdoors, algae needs to be grown year-round in a warm, sunny climate. Only about 10 percent of the land in the United States could provide such a climate, and most of that land is in the deserts of the Southwest. Water is another necessity, and it is especially scarce in the desert. While algae does not need fresh drinking water, it does need plenty of water. Proponents say that algae can be grown in brackish or polluted water, as well as seawater. But critics say that systems to pump brackish water up from desert groundwater or networks of pipelines running seawater to the desert are very expensive. Ponds often have to be lined to meet groundwater regulatory requirements, and this is also expensive.

Supporters of algal biodiesel believe that a very important win-win situation is to grow algae in wastewater. In wastewater plants, algae not only grows quickly, but it also absorbs unwanted chemicals such as nitrogen and phosphorus, preventing the need for treatment plants to filter them out. However, Dr. Benemann disagrees, saying, "What people don't understand is that the market for algae for wastewater treatment is quite limited. For very simple reasons, like you need land and where you have lots of people and lots of municipal wastewater, you don't often have a lot of land."

When algae is grown outdoors, the serious problem of contamination often arises. Contamination comes from other, unwanted algae, as well as viruses, bacteria, and fungi. When algae is contaminated, it turns from green to brown or black in just a few days, dying off until there is only water left. Professor Qiang Hu, who heads the Arizona State University algae research team, says that "the number one challenge the emerging algae industry faces today is algal culture protection. Without solving this problem, you won't have an industry for biofuels." To combat unwanted algae from taking over the biofuel algae crop, growers must spend money to cover the ponds. Also, to comply with US EPA water regulations, the bottoms of open ponds and trenches must be lined to prevent leakage into nearby groundwater.

Closed Systems

Many algal biofuel producers have chosen to grow their crops in containers, bioreactors, greenhouses, and photo-bioreactors. The prime benefit in closed systems is the ability to control contamination and to recycle water use. Studies have shown it is possible to grow ten times more algae in a bioreactor than in an open pond. Yet there are numerous problems with closed systems. First of all, building the structures is very expensive. They require plumbing, pumps, special mixtures of carbon dioxide, and other substances. In the instance of closed containers and

Vertical bioreactor systems that grow algae must pump in CO_2, sugar, and fertilizers and require advanced lighting technologies to work properly.

bioreactors, there is also the need for costly high-tech panels that mimic sunlight. Additionally, the tanks and reactors need to be cleaned frequently and the temperature must be controlled. No matter which crop-growing method is used, algae producers need to achieve a balance between growing their crop quickly versus the high cost of maintaining their systems.

Processing and Harvesting

In all forms of harvesting, a producer must skim wet algae, whether in a pond, a container, or a bioreactor. Then the wet, gluey algae has to be scraped from the skimmer or filters. It is difficult and expensive to build and operate such machinery on a large scale. Each type of algae and

A DEEPER DIVE

Is It All Worth It?

Algae biofuel is expensive to produce and fossil fuel prices are still sufficiently low. Oil prices worldwide have dropped, and more and more countries are conserving energy, using alternative energies, and driving fuel-efficient vehicles that run on electricity, hydrogen, and natural gas. Meanwhile, in the United States and some other countries, the new method of hydraulic fracking that unleashes huge reserves of domestic oil and natural gas has helped to ease the demand for foreign fossil fuels. According to a study by the Lawrence Berkeley National Laboratory, producing "green crude" oil from algae ponds currently costs nearly 200 percent more than petroleum crude oil.

A DEEPER DIVE

The Fine Print

Reading the ingredients on a box of cereal, for example, turns up a lot of fine print about what goes into the cereal besides oats and honey. Algae biofuels also have "fine print" ingredients. Besides carbon dioxide, algae also needs to be fed phosphorus, ammonia, and other chemicals. If these fertilizers escape the open ponds and trenches, they can pollute both surface and ground water. Fertilizers, such as phosphorus and ammonia, are at least 30 percent of the cost of operating an algae farm.

Burning algal biodiesel also carries "fine print" about what comes out of the exhaust pipe. Although algal biodiesel produces lower amounts of carbon dioxide and emits fewer particles in the air than standard diesel, algal biodiesel emits an increased amount of nitrogen oxide (NOx) gases. NOx gases are formed when fuel, such as biodiesel, is burned at high temperatures. When large quantities of NOx come into contact with sunlight, they form acid rain and smog. Half of all NOx emissions come from vehicles.

This biodiesel refinery in France required an investment of more than $40 million to construct. Critics say that the current costs to manufacture biodiesel are too high.

each type of growing environment needs its own specialized equipment. After the algae is collected, it has to be dried, either naturally or in a heated space. Only then can oil extraction take place. Depending on how much the crude oil will be refined—lubricating oil, fuel oil, biodiesel, or bioethanol—the algae has to be separated into its parts: oil and proteins.

Most of the processing requires extreme temperatures and chemicals. While there are several mechanical ways of separating the algae to extract the oil, the most common way to make biodiesel is a process called **transesterification**, where the algae is combined with chemicals such as methanol and lye. One effective and inexpensive chemical is benzene; however, benzene is a hazardous chemical and can be very harmful to workers. There are problems with other chemicals, too, as some carry the risk of explosion. *Science* magazine reported the research of two biofuels experts who concluded that "current processes for turning algae oil into biodiesel are not efficient enough or on a large enough scale to create the amount of algal biofuel required to replace fossil fuel. In order for algal biofuel to replace fossil fuels, it will have to become cheaper to produce and a great deal of infrastructure will have to be built to process the volume that will be required." Dr. Krassen Dimitrov, a leading bioengineer, commented, "People need to understand that in energy we cannot expect dramatic changes overnight."

Energy and the Environment

If algal and other biofuels are going to rescue the planet from pollution, they must be environmentally friendly and use energy efficiently. Algae is a more environmentally friendly crop to grow than soybeans and corn, which require water and fertilizer and heavy farm machinery. There are concerns, however, that the fastest, most productive algae need fertilizer, much of which is made from petroleum. Many scientists report that the best algae is not wild algae but genetically engineered algae. Environmentalists worry that the altered algae could escape containment,

Open pond "raceways" are the least expensive way to grow algae but are always at risk for contamination to the crop and to the surrounding native environment.

causing harm to the environment and damaging wild algae species. Additionally, algae does not in itself reduce CO_2 in the atmosphere. Rather, algae just absorbs and holds onto it. When the algae dies, it gives off CO_2. The only way algae reduces CO_2 in the environment is if it is burned in place of fossil fuels, which emit greater amounts of CO_2

than algal biofuels. Supporters of algae say that algae can be grown near factories to help reduce CO_2, but other experts say that it not only costs money to pipe the CO_2 into the algae fields but that it would take thousands of acres of algae to absorb the CO_2 from a large power plant.

In an interview with researchers from the National Academy of Sciences Research Council, one researcher commented:

> You have a fair bit of energy that is required to actually just cultivate the algae to keep them suspended and moving in the water. You have a fair bit of energy in removing the algae from the water itself in that collection. And then you have the processing energy of breaking the algae open to get the oils out. And it takes a bit more energy to turn the oils into fuel. And then there's land. An acre [0.4 ha] of algae ponds would produce enough fuel to supply maybe ten cars.

Research

Research has a long road ahead. A big problem with making affordable algal biofuel occurs in the research laboratory itself. Since the 1970s, laboratories have shown that it is possible to produce algal biofuels to operate vehicles and machinery. However, what works in the laboratory does not translate to affordable, large-scale algal biofuel production. Only a few companies are building test farms and developing ideal methods of harvesting and producing. None so far have developed cost-effective means of producing algal fuels. Algae biofuel research has received money from the US government, but to be successful it will need funding

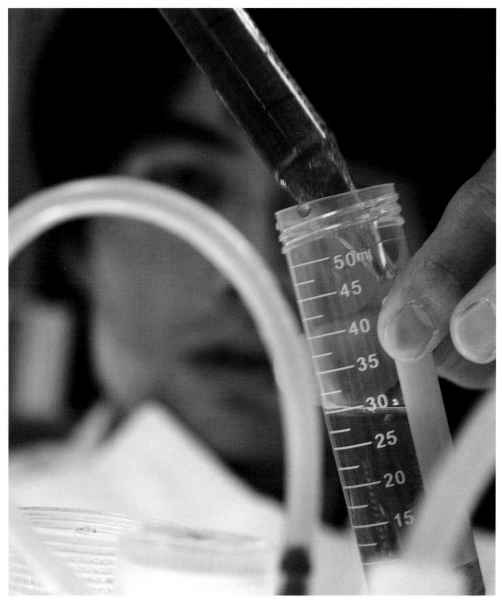

Critics say that algae research that yields positive results is done on such a small scale that the methods may not necessarily translate into effective large-scale production.

from businesses and investors to create large-scale fuel production. Jeremy Martin, a senior scientist at the Union of Concerned Scientists' clean vehicles program writes, "When it comes to algae, it's a science project that's worth pursuing, but there are no guarantees as to when it might be considered or what scale it might find use."

Many new algal biofuel companies are excited about their prospects, but their critics, especially in the agriculture industry, say algae is nowhere near able to replace vegetable-based ethanol for efficiency and economy. In an article titled "Algae 2020," researcher Will Thurmond states, "In actuality, it really isn't that easy, and the volume of biofuel from algae that could make a difference in oil imports or replacing corn-based ethanol appears to be years away. Already, algae energy companies have come and gone. Only a handful of companies seem to have technology that matches even part of their companies' vision."

A recent study from the University of Texas said energy and fuel production of algae is far from ready to go to market. The study said that it is possible algae could eventually produce five hundred times more energy than it takes to grow it while oil and gas make about thirty to forty times as much energy as it takes to produce. But, the researchers at the university say, algae currently only produces one five-hundredth of the amount of energy that it takes to make it.

Driving on Algae

People who want to drive biofuel to help protect the environment and reduce the United States' dependence on oil from the Middle East can run into problems using algal biofuel. The Department of Energy reports,

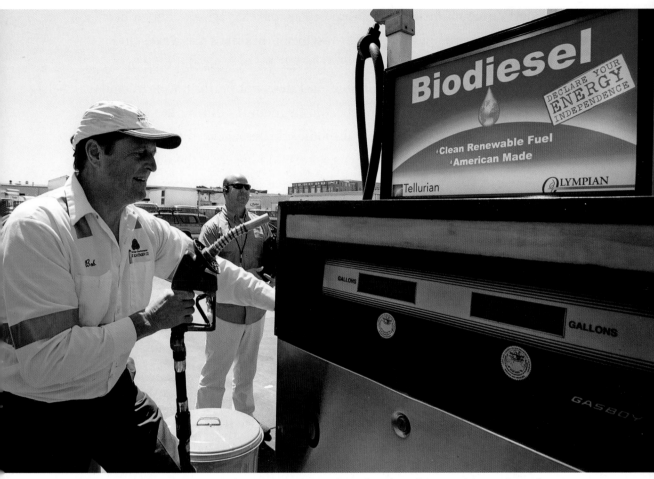

During a pilot project on the West Coast, algae biodiesel was sold at selected locations. Many drivers reported that their diesel cars ran smoother and had better mileage than when using petroleum diesel.

"The initial use of B20 or B100 [B20 is a blend of 20 percent biodiesel and 80 percent diesel, and B100 is 100 percent biodiesel] in any vehicle or machine requires care." Algal biofuels are oily, and while they can help keep an engine clean, they can also stir up problems in the fuel system. Petroleum diesel forms deposits of waxes, crystals, and sticky slime in the engine and fuel lines. Biodiesel dissolves the waxes and gooey deposits, which then migrate through the system and clog fuel lines, pumps, and filters. Algal biodiesel does not perform well in cold weather, which is a problem for most of the country during the winter months. In older diesel cars, algal biodiesel runs hotter than standard diesel and can break down rubber gaskets and hoses in the engine compartment. Many people who want to drive algal biofuels have to pay to modify their engines and in doing so may lose their vehicle warranties. Algal biodiesel also has a reduced performance compared to standard diesel as well as a reduced fuel economy. Lastly, algal biofuels are not readily available in the United States, and building a nationwide distribution network would be extremely costly.

CRITICAL THINKING

- Describe the kind of algae-growing system that would be likely chosen for your hometown. Why?

- Many scientists seem to say that biofuels are a good idea to help reduce the amount of fossil fuels that are burned. However, do you think more money should go into creating a whole new system based on algal biodiesel, including buying more diesel cars? Or should more efforts go into improving established biofuels, such as ethanol made from corn or sugar beets?

Drivers can usually put lower biodiesel blends in their diesel cars, but anything more than 20 percent requires engine modifications.

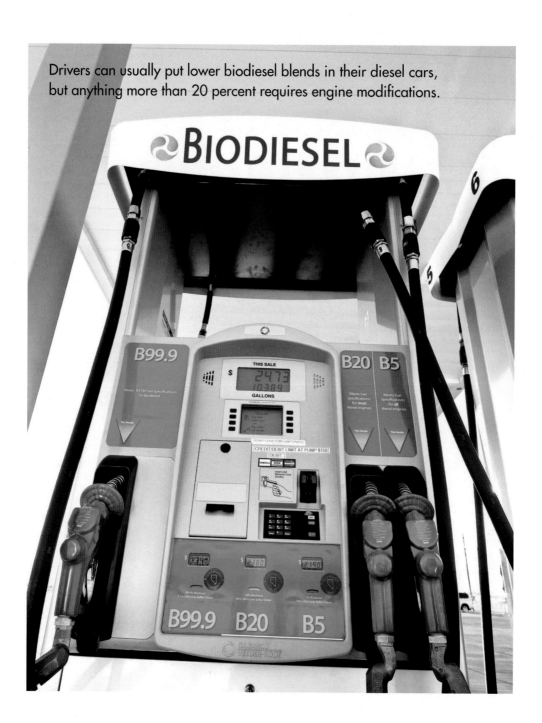

Chapter 4

Going Green

Citizens around the world recognize that our supply of fossil fuels will not last. Most fear that burning fossil fuels is damaging Earth's climate. World politics has an important role in determining the cost and the availability of fossil fuels. Few doubt that there is a need to develop alternate sources of renewable energy. Many scientists, energy experts, environmentalists, transportation companies, biofuel organizations, and governments are supporting the development of algae-based biofuels as a means of solving the problem of fossil fuels.

Stalking Corn

Rudolf Diesel believed his vegetable oil–run biodiesel engine would have the added benefit of giving more farmers jobs. Today, many believe that farmers growing food crops to make ethanol may be causing more harm than good. Instead of reducing carbon in the atmosphere, they are using more energy plowing up new fields. Supporters of algal biofuels say that corn, sugar beets, soybeans, and other crops used for ethanol production take away valuable land that should be used to grow food. By reducing the amount of crops grown for food, food prices go up, not only in the United States but throughout the world. In many impoverished areas of the world, prices for basic foods such as wheat or corn have doubled. In the United States, 40 percent of the corn crop is grown to make fuel for cars. "Ethanol uses 4.9 billion bushels of corn in the US," says Lester Brown, president of the Earth Policy Institute. "That's enough grain to feed 350 million people." Corn farmers, however, fear a loss of income without support for ethanol crops. Supporters of algal biofuels suggest that farmers who want to grow energy crops could make greater profits switching from field crops to algae growing. Algae-based biofuels produce more fuel on less land, and furthermore, they can be grown on poor-quality land unsuitable for other crops. According to a study by the US Department of Energy, if algae producers were to make enough biofuel to replace fossil fuels, they would need around 15,000 square miles (38,850 square kilometers), roughly the size of the small state of Maryland. However, if soybeans or corn were to replace fossil fuels, the land required would be nearly the size of half the entire United States. Supporters of algal biofuel say that if more effort, research, and financing went toward algae-based fuels, more farmers, especially farmers who do not have large farms, could turn to growing algae to earn a good living.

Each year, the EPA establishes a Renewable Fuels Standard (RFS), which decides how much biofuel must be mixed into the fossil fuels used in vehicles. In 2014, the RFS was 14 billion gallons (53 billion L). Many ethanol farmers are disturbed because the RFS for corn and soybean ethanol has been decreasing lately. "The EPA still supports ethanol, but it wants to take some of the focus off corn, and put it back on greener ways of making ethanol," reports Grant Gerlock of Nebraska Public

Radio. The EPA now is calling for more use of "advanced biofuels," which are non-food biofuels such as algae-based fuels. In 2014, the EPA RFS for advanced biofuels and non-food biodiesel was 3.5 billion gallons (13.2 billion L), an increase over past years. Additionally, the EPA is making changes to requirements for commercial airplane emissions and has already certified algae-based jet fuel made by three algae biofuel companies. The EPA is encouraging more energy companies to invest in renewable, low-carbon fuels—such as algae—that are made from crops other than corn.

Research

John Benemann calls algae an interesting field of research. He says algae research can yield quick results because the plant grows so fast that many experiments can have results almost overnight, whereas for other plants, researchers must wait out a long growing season. To understand the effects of new technology, scientists must study several generations of plants. For a crop such as corn, that is several years, but for algae, it can take as little as a month. Algae can also be studied on a smaller scale, and because it can be grown in so many types of environments, there can be fewer locations. One of the biggest arguments about laboratory experiments in algae technology, however, is that the experiments are in fact small and do not necessarily work in actual large-scale production. Vinod Khasla, an investor in biofuels, tells algal biofuel companies, "If it doesn't scale, then it doesn't matter."

The Department of Energy's Bioenergy Technologies Office (BETO) supports "the development of technologies to sustainably grow and

A researcher at NREL experiments with speeding up the process of growing algae in controlled conditions.

convert algae into advanced biofuels." The office hopes to soon see production of 5 billion gallons (19 billion L) of algal biofuel a year. On the other hand, Mark Wigmosta, a PNNL water expert, says, "I'm confident that algal biofuels can be part of the solution to our energy needs, but algal biofuels certainly aren't the whole solution." He points out that the current cost of making algal biofuel far exceeds the cost of producing traditional gasoline-based products.

Government Support

The US government has supported research of algal biofuels at the National Aeronautics and Space Administration (NASA) and at several of its seventeen national laboratories, especially the National Renewable Energy Laboratory (NREL), Pacific Northwest National Laboratory (PNNL), Idaho National Laboratory (INL), and the Oak Ridge National Laboratory (ORNL). In 2015, the NREL discovered that a certain combination of iron and sulfur in algae could make hydrogen, which is

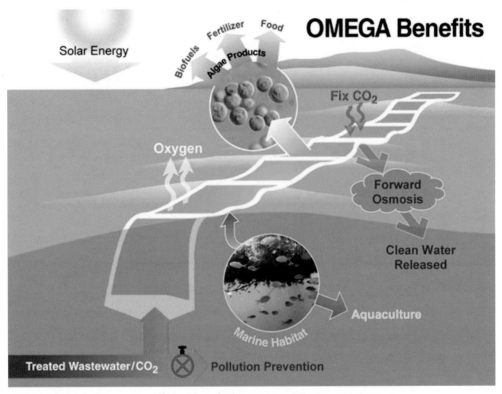

This diagram shows the life cycle of algae growing in wastewater.

A DEEPER DIVE

Major Players

ALGEON
Location: **Florida and New Mexico**
Technologies: **Saltwater, photo-bioreactor, extracting CO_2 from power plants**
Products: **Ethanol, biodiesel, and jet fuel**

SAPPHIRE ENERGY
Location: **Las Cruces, New Mexico**
Technology: **Open ponds**
Product: **"Green crude" (which is refined in existing processing plants into ethanol, biodiesel, and bio–jet fuel)**

SOLAZYME
Location: Headquarters: San Francisco, California;
facility: Peoria, Illinois
Technology: Bio-refinery
Products: Jet fuel (US Air Force), marine biodiesel
(US Navy), lubricants

SOLIX BIOFUELS
Location: Coyote Gulch, Colorado
Technology: Vertical panels outdoors
Product: Biodiesel, green diesel, bio–jet fuels

Alternative aviation fuels, including algae jet fuel, were the highlight of the 2015 Paris Air Show.

another hopeful source of renewable energy. Researchers there called another experiment "feed and starve." They learned that if they starved algae of nitrogen after feeding it CO_2, nitrogen, and sunlight, the algae would become a "couch potato," meaning it would stop growing and instead start storing fat. Using this technique, growers could produce more oil with less algae. At PNNL, researchers were able to pump wet algae into a chemical reactor that spat out crude oil in just an hour, as well as by-products, including phosphorus, that could be reused as fertilizer in another crop of algae. PNNL researchers have stated, "Approximately 17 percent of fossil fuel imported into the United States for transportation purposes could be replaced by algae biofuel by as early as 2020." Some experts say that figure is low. The ORNL is focusing on hydrogen-fueled cars and is testing blue-green algae to produce hydrogen. The INL is working with an algae oil company to develop a high-speed algae separator that does not use chemicals.

One of the ways in which the government supports energy production is through **subsidies**, or financial grants. Some subsidies are for research, some for conservation programs, and others are direct subsidies to producers so that they can sell their fuel to consumers at a lower cost. In 2013, the government spent $16 billion assisting energy technology and production. Nearly 45 percent of the money was given to renewable energy sources, with the rest going to fossil fuel and nuclear energy companies. Wyoming congresswoman Cynthia Lummis stated before Congress, "Government should work to ensure that Americans have access to abundant, affordable, reliable energy, and target taxpayer resources to fundamental research that could one day enable these technologies to compete without expensive subsidies or mandates. Doing so would not only help bring energy independence and grow our economy, but it would bring revenue to the Treasury." It is clear the government wants to see renewable energy play a larger role in serving the nation's energy needs, and by including support for algae biofuel laboratories and production

A DEEPER DIVE

The Green Fleet

In October 2010, the US Navy began purchasing algae biofuel for its Nimitz-class war ships. Original costs were very expensive, but costs today are decreasing as production is increasing. Since 2008, the navy has worked with private companies to develop algal marine biofuels for its "Green Strike Force" and jet fuel for its fighter jets. The navy hopes that developing algae as a reliable fuel will protect the navy from being at the mercy of foreign governments who can radically raise prices or cut off supplies. One of the most appealing features of algal fuels to the navy is that it is a "drop-in fuel." To the navy, a drop-in fuel means they can simply fill the ships' fuel tanks and set sail. There is no need to modify their engines. One officer explained that when the navy attempted to use ethanol as a fuel, it filled the tanks, but the ship could only go half as far. But not so with algal marine diesel.

It is true that the cost of algal biofuels still remains much higher than fossil fuels, but the secretary of the navy stated, "Simply put, we as a military rely too much on fossil fuels." An assistant deputy secretary explained, "We purchase fuels today from some parts of the world that are not very friendly to the US. Having sources to replace those unfriendly fuel barrels with domestically grown fuel barrels is important." On the other hand, there are citizens who are angered over the use of taxpayers' money being spent on unproven fuels.

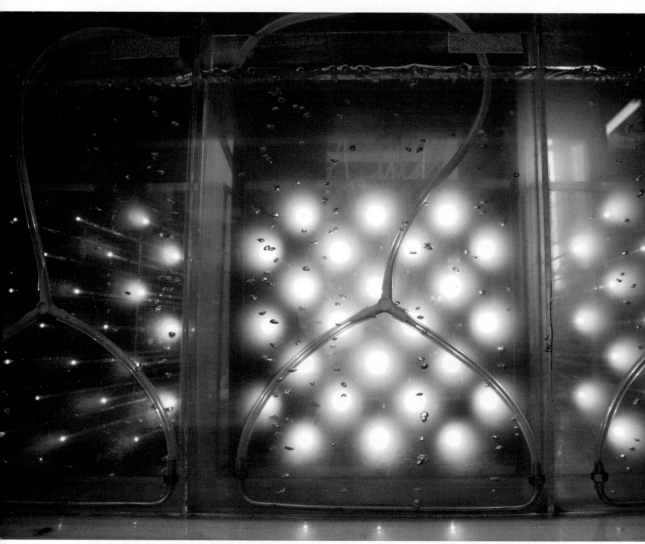

Sunlight streams through a solar collector that is being used to grow oilier, faster-growing algae in a government-sponsored experiment at Utah State University.

companies, the government believes algae biofuels will become a valuable energy resource. No one expects algal biofuel or any other renewable biofuel to take over from fossil fuels in the immediate future, but even today, biofuels are gaining in their ability to reduce dependency on fossil fuels. The government has long subsidized new technologies, and today the government is showing its support for algal biofuels.

Military Might

The military has a goal of getting at least 25 percent of its energy from renewable energy sources by 2020. The US Department of Defense's Defense Advanced Research Projects Agency (DARPA) is very enthusiastic about algae becoming a major renewable fuel source. Through its research, the agency has been able to extract oil from algae ponds at a cost of $2 per gallon ($0.53 per L). Presently, DARPA research is going into large-scale processing of algae, which is costing about $3 per gallon ($0.79 per L). The Department of Defense wants to reduce the military's use of oil, which equals close to 75 million barrels a year (3.15 billion gal or 11.9 billion L). Much of that oil goes to fighter jets and military cargo planes. Algae fuels designed for aircraft contain about 10 percent more energy than standard jet fuel. Military energy experts note that planes flying on algae-based fuels will be able to fly farther with the same amount of fuel in their tanks.

Pressure to make algae fuel more available also comes from commanders in war zones. Transporting fossil fuels, whether by air or by truck, is not only costly but dangerous. Commanders say that by producing their own fuel in the field they could limit the transportation

A DEEPER DIVE

The Veggie Van

In 2009, the movie *Fuel* won the award for best director at the Sundance Film Festival. The director, Josh Tickell, grew up in an oil-producing region and saw firsthand some of the environmental problems associated with extracting and burning fossil fuels. He believes algae will be an important player in the race for replacing fossil fuels. He said that because the government is putting billions of dollars behind developing algae fuels, "We can expect to see major breakthroughs on algae within the next five years." His movie included many celebrities who agreed that the nation needs to move toward safe, clean, renewable energy, such as Woody Harrelson, Julia Roberts, Sheryl Crow, Larry Hagman, Robert Kennedy Jr., Larry David, Willie Nelson, and

BIOFUELS
ENDORSED BY
EE©A
Energy Efficiency and
Conservation Authority

bío
FUEL

CONTAINS UP TO 10% ETHANOL

May not be suitable for
all vehicles / engines.

Check with your
manufacturer before use.

Neil Young. Actor Woody Harrelson drove his "veggie van" running on biofuel across the country and gave speeches about the need to develop biofuels. At the film's opening, a caravan of high-tech "green" vehicles began a ten-day tour from San Francisco to New York City, led by the "Algaeus," an algae-powered Toyota Prius. "People think of algae fuel as this long-term, far off thing," Harrelson said. "But seeing is believing."

Many branches of the US military are studying new ways to develop algae biofuel for its vehicles, planes, and ships, including the US Navy and DARPA.

of fuel, making soldiers safer and field operations more efficient. Barbara McQuiston of DARPA explains that by producing algal biofuels in the field, the military would not only be able to provide its own fuel, but it would be able to leave the people of the region with sustainable fuel production facilities once the military departed. McQuiston is hopeful about the success of the research, pointing out that many useful things that are part of everyday life were once created by the military, such as the Internet and GPS satellite navigation systems. "Everyone is well aware that a lot of things were started in the military," she said. If military research could produce cost-effective algal biofuel, it would be a "game-changer."

Keep on Trucking

Diesel-powered passenger cars and trucks are the main potential users of algal biofuel. Paul Woods is a founder of an algal biofuel company that makes fuel for airplanes and is now experimenting on making isobutyl alcohol from algae. Isobutyl alcohol is more energy efficient than ethanol and can be blended into gasoline. It is also an ingredient in making biodiesel. Although algae can produce algal ethanol, isobutyl alcohol, hydrogen, and biodiesel, most companies are focusing on biodiesel. Algal biodiesel takes fewer steps to refine than ethanol and can be blended with diesel or used on its own in diesel engines. Diesel engines are 35 percent more efficient, use less energy to refine their fuel, and do not emit unpleasant odors with new technologies available. Of all biofuels, algal biodiesel is the only one to have passed emissions tests established by the Clean Air Act. Almost all commercial trucks and vans run on diesel fuel, and because biodiesel has fewer emissions than standard diesel, the EPA is regulating that they must use more biodiesel. However, a big issue is how few diesel passenger cars are made or imported into the United States. In Europe, a much higher percentage of cars have diesel engines. Supporters of algal biodiesel want to see more diesel passenger cars on American roads.

Major oil companies such as Chevron, Exxon, and BP are researching and investing in algae-based biodiesel fuels. One journalist remembers the "heady times in the 1980s when oil companies invested a lot of money in algae research. It's like we put a message in a bottle and sent it out to sea. Now it's coming back, and that's pretty exciting." But foreign and domestic oil prices dropped dramatically in 2015, and the hydrofracking of new reserves of oil has made fossil fuels much cheaper. Many supporters see an unfortunate lull in algal research and development, causing momentum to shift. Yet oil companies and other biofuel companies are still at work. One government researcher says, "They're investigating all the pathways … looking for the most cost-effective method." Although a long way into the future, people know that there will be a time when the world's supply of oil is exhausted. As one algae supporter pointed out, "The world can't grind to a halt for a decade or two while the next fuel is developed and implemented."

Many biofuel experts say that algae biofuels are a perfect choice for producing renewable energy. Algae grows fifty to one hundred times faster than food crops grown for ethanol and can produce more fuel per acre. Algae-based biofuels are more energy efficient and absorb more carbon dioxide than they give off. Algae is plentiful and can grow almost anywhere. Although detractors say that commercial use of algae is a long way into the future and may never arrive, governments, universities, research laboratories, and hundreds of companies around the world are betting that algal biofuels will fuel our cars, clean our planet, and may someday replace fossil fuels altogether. In 2012, President Obama awarded a research grant to a Florida company producing algae-based jet fuel saying, "We're making new investments in the development of gasoline and diesel and jet fuel that's actually made from a plant-like substance—algae … If we can figure out how to make energy out of that, we'll be doing all right."

CRITICAL THINKING

- If you wanted the fastest and most effective way for more drivers to fill their tanks with algal biofuels, would you focus on producing algal ethanol (or isobutyl alcohol) that can be blended into gasoline, or biodiesel, which does not necessarily have to be blended with diesel? Why?

- What do you think would encourage more gas stations to offer algal biodiesel or biodiesel blends—appealing to drivers who already own diesel vehicles to ask for it or appealing to automakers to produce more diesel vehicles?

Glossary

algae Simple nonflowering plants that lack roots, stems, or leaves.

barrels (of oil) A measurement of petroleum oil. One barrel = 42 gallons (159 liters).

biofuels Fuels made from plants or animals.

bioreactor A device in which a biological reaction or process is carried out, especially in industry.

carbon dioxide A colorless, odorless gas produced by burning carbon and organic compounds and by respiration.

carbon footprint The amount of greenhouse gases, specifically carbon dioxide, emitted by an organization, event, product, or person.

centrifuge A machine with a rapidly rotating container that applies centrifugal force to its contents, typically to separate fluids of different densities or liquids from solids.

chlorophyll A green pigment, present in all green plants, responsible for absorbing sunlight to provide energy for photosynthesis.

diesel A high temperature fuel used in diesel engines, which use pressure to ignite the fuel.

ethanol An alcohol made from fermenting sugars that is a flammable liquid.

fossil fuel A natural fuel, such as coal, oil, or gas, formed in the geological past from the remains of living organisms.

greenhouse gases Gases in Earth's atmosphere, such as carbon dioxide, methane, nitrous oxide, and ozone, that absorb the sun's radiation and trap heat in the atmosphere.

lipids Organic molecules that are fatty acids, such as oil and wax, that are insoluble in water but can be dissolved in organic solvents, such as alcohol.

nitrogen A chemical element that is a colorless, odorless, unreactive gas that forms about 78 percent of Earth's atmosphere.

phosphorus An element that combines with other elements that can be toxic and/or flammable. It is key to the growth of plants.

subsidies Money granted by the government or a public body to help an industry or business to keep prices affordable for consumers.

sustainable An adjective describing methods that do not completely use up or destroy natural resources.

transesterification A chemical process that separates lipid fat molecules with alcohol.

ultrasonic Rapid vibrations similar to sound waves.

Find Out More

Books

Arato, Rona. *Protists: Algae, Amoebas, Plankton, and Other Protists.* A Class of Their Own. New York: Crabtree Publishing, 2010.

Hamilton, Tyler, ed. *Mad Like Tesla: Underdog Inventors and their Relentless Pursuit of Clean Energy.* Toronto, ON: ECW Press, 2011.

Haven, Kendall. *Green Electricity: 25 Green Technologies That Will Electrify Your Future.* Westport, CT: Libraries Unlimited, 2011.

Websites

All About Algae
www.allaboutalgae.com

This informative website includes the history, biology, and benefits of algal biofuels, as well as explanations of farming and production systems.

Green Car Reports: NASA Ready to Show Off Algae Biofuel Research Project
www.greencarreports.com/news/1075546_nasa-ready-to-show-off-algae-biofuel-research-project

This article describes NASA's Project OMEGA (Offshore Membrane Enclosures for Growing Algae), which is growing algae in seawater to produce algal biofuels, including jet fuel.

How Stuff Works: Algae Biofuels

science.howstuffworks.com/environmental/green-science/algae-biodiesel.htm

Several articles discuss algae as biofuel, including what is algae, how it is farmed, pros and cons, and how biodiesel works. You can even take an "Algae Fact or Fiction?" quiz.

Smithsonian: Scientists Turn Algae Into Crude Oil
In Less Than An Hour

www.smithsonianmag.com/innovation/scientists-turn-algae-into-crude-oil-in-less-than-an-hour-180948282

This article describes how the Pacific Northwest National Laboratory (PNNL) turned a small mixture of algae and water into crude oil in less than an hour.

US Department of Energy: Algal Biofuels

energy.gov/eere/bioenergy/algal-biofuels

This site provides an introduction to the Department of Energy's report on algae biofuels. Click on the link to the National Renewable Energy Laboratory for a video explaining their algae-to-biofuels process.

Index

Page numbers in **boldface** are illustrations. Entries in **boldface** are glossary terms.

About the Author

Ruth Bjorklund received a master's degree in library and information science from the University of Washington in Seattle. Her home is on Bainbridge Island, a thirty-minute ferry ride away from Seattle. She and her family live by a bay where they enjoy swimming, kayaking, and sailing together. After researching algae as a source of alternative energy, Bjorklund looks at the occasional algae blooms in the bay in a whole new light.

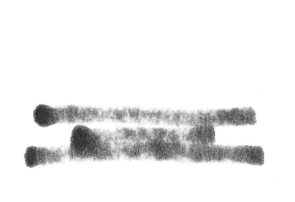

12/16